Sound

Contents

What is sound?

We cannot see sound but we know it exists because we can hear it and, sometimes, we can feel it. Sound is a bit like the wind. We cannot see the wind but we can feel it on our faces and see it moving the leaves on the trees. If you stand on the edge of a large field of tall grass you may see the wind blowing the stalks. This makes them move. Their movements are like waves travelling to and fro across the field. Sound moves in waves too but we cannot see them.

Sounds are made by some kind of movement. It might be your fingers tapping on the table or a cat scratching at the door with its paw. These movements cause vibrations to travel through the air. We call these travelling vibrations **sound waves**. The sound waves move tiny particles of air which bump into each other. We hear loud sounds when moving particles bump together with a lot of force or energy. We hear quieter sounds when they hit each other more weakly, or with less force.

There is no sound in outer space because there is no air in outer space. Without air, there can be no sound vibrations.

Loud or soft?

Some sounds are loud, some sounds are quiet. Taking crisps out of a bag can sound loud, or it can sound quiet. It depends where you are! If you are sitting in a quiet cinema, rustling a bag will sound very noisy, but if you are in a football crowd, no one will hear it!

What loud and quiet sounds can you think of? A simple action, like screwing up a paper bag, can make many different sounds. Try squeezing a bag very slowly and very carefully. Try again, quickly and vigorously. What do you notice about the differences in sound? What happens if you blow up the bag and burst it? The stronger the vibrations, the louder the sound.

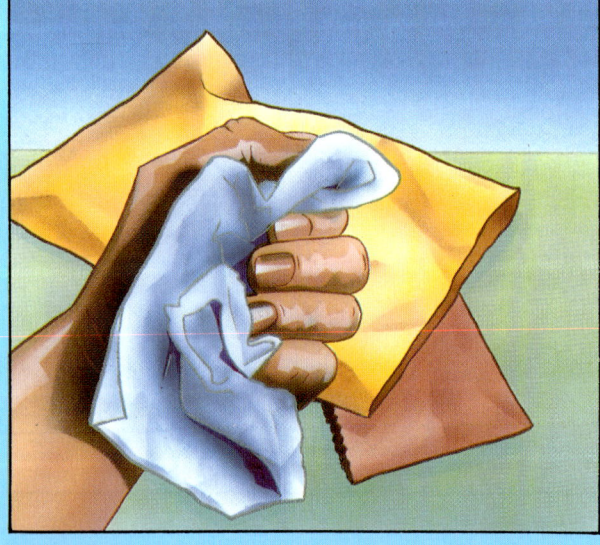

Feeling sound

If you have ever been to a concert where the music was very loud, you may have felt the sound vibrations.

All musicians use vibrations to help them make music. It is possible for deaf people to play rhythms on percussion instruments by feeling the vibrations through their bodies.

The composer, Beethoven, became deaf. He used to put his ear to the piano to feel the vibrations of the wood. In this way, he continued to compose music and play the piano for many years after he became deaf.

Blow up a balloon and hold it to one ear. Scratch the balloon. What can you feel? The air inside the balloon vibrates and you can feel it on the other side of the balloon.

Put some dried peas or some sand on the skin of a drum and beat the drum. What happens to the peas or sand? Why?

Strike a tuning fork so that it makes a sound. Touch the surface of a bowl of water with the end of one of the prongs. What happens to the water?

Can you think of any other ways to see or feel sound vibrations?

How do we hear?

Our ears are like funnels. They are specially shaped to collect sound waves.

1 Ear drum
Vibrations in the air pass down the funnel to the ear drum. This is a thin skin stretched tightly across the end. The skin vibrates like a drum.

2 Hammer, anvil and stirrup
These three tiny bones vibrate too.

Hammer
Anvil
Stirrup

4 Hearing nerve
The electrical messages travel along the hearing nerve to the brain where they are understood.

3 Cochlea
The bones pass the sound to a snail-shaped tube filled with liquid and tiny hairs. These turn the vibrations into electrical messages.

Light travels faster than sound. You see a flash of lightning before you hear thunder although they both happen at the same time.

Animals' ears

Animals have ears that are different from our own. Every animal has ears which are perfect for its needs.

Mice have ears high up on their heads. Their ears contain muscles which can move them in different directions to catch the smallest sounds. Mice need good hearing so that they can hear cats and other enemies.

Like mice, cats can also move their ears. The tiniest rustle in long grass will make their ears twitch in the right direction.

Some dogs have ears which stand up. Others have floppy ears. Spaniels' large ear flaps protect the insides of their ears from sharp thorns and nettles in thick undergrowth. They love to swim and their ear flaps help keep the water out. Spaniels can move their ears. They lift up slightly when they hear a noise. Can you move your ears too?

Common seals have no ears that we can see. Muscles close the entrance to their ears when they dive underwater. Sea-lions have ears that we can see.

Making sounds

These musical instruments make different sounds. The guitar makes a different type of sound to the drum; the piano makes a different sort of sound to the recorder. Try playing some instruments. Can you describe the different sounds the musical instruments make?

You can play high and low notes on each of these instruments too. Can you sing some high and low notes? The highness or lowness of a note is called its **pitch**. The high pitched notes of the piano are at the right-hand end of the keyboard. The low pitched notes are at the left-hand end. Try making some differently pitched notes on various musical instruments.

Percussion instruments

Percussion instruments make sounds when they are struck or shaken. The sound that they make can be varied by the type of stick that you hit them with. The sound also depends on the material that the instrument itself is made of.

A drum is a hollow box with a skin stretched tightly across. If you beat it with wooden sticks, it makes a sharp sound. Softer sounds can be made by using sticks with felt on the end or by using brushes.

Each of the wooden bars on a xylophone makes a different sound. How are the bars different? What is it about them that makes each one sound different?

Make a xylophone using pieces of wood of different sizes. Try making different sounds with your xylophone by hitting it with different beaters. Record the sounds you make with different beaters.

Stringed instruments

Instruments which belong to the string family have two main parts. The strings make the sounds and the hollow box under the strings makes the sounds louder. The hollow box also helps give the strings of a particular instrument their own special sound.

Guitar strings are plucked. Violins are usually played with a **bow**. On both instruments, the strings are stretched across a sound box. The vibrating strings make the air inside the box vibrate too. Sound boxes of different shapes and sizes give different types of sounds. A small violin does not sound like a big double bass, even though the shape looks quite similar.

Stroh violins were made without sound boxes. They had a metal horn attached to the frame to boost the sound waves. The sound was not very pleasant though, so they are no longer made.

Experiment with some string and elastic bands to make different sounds. Can you make sounds of different pitch from the same elastic band? What did you do to the elastic band to make noises of different pitch?

Can you make a musical instrument with four differently pitched notes from an empty tissue box and four elastic bands?

Wind instruments

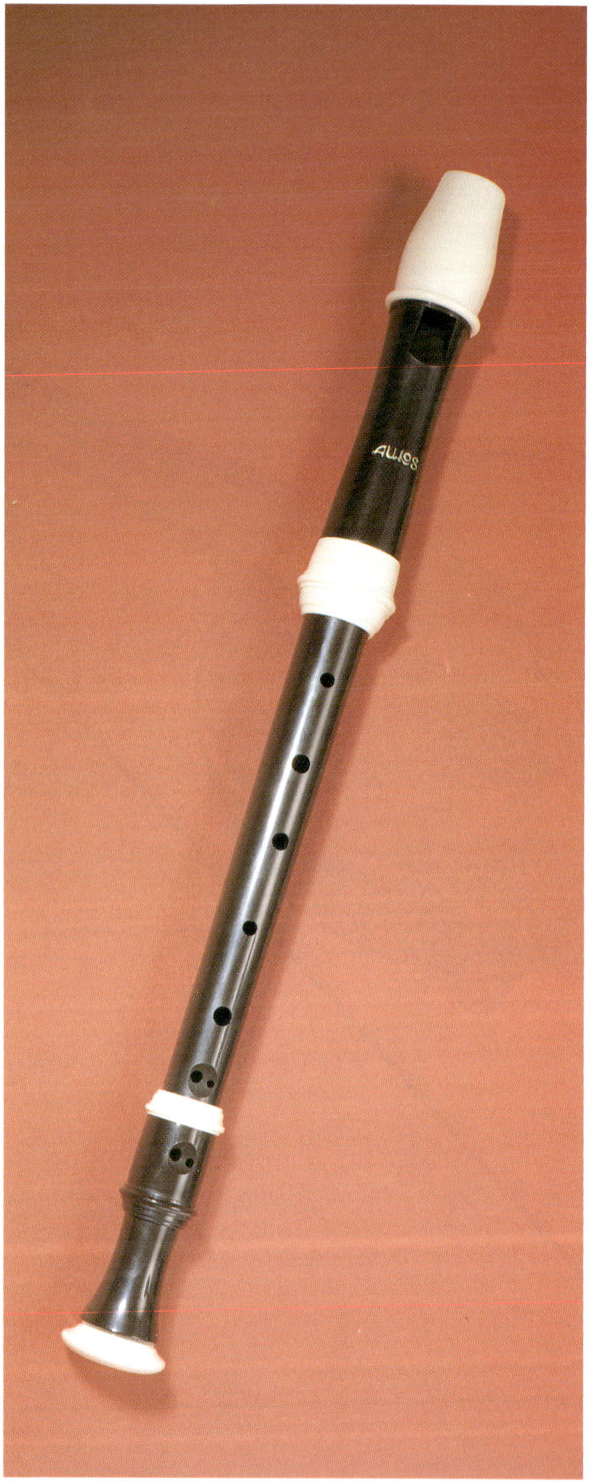

You blow into a wind instrument to make a sound. Your breath makes a column of air inside the instrument vibrate. The vibrations produce a note. The air is made to vibrate by blowing across a sharp edge. In a recorder, there is a notch cut out below the mouthpiece. When you blow a recorder, your breath hits the sharp edge of the notch and makes the column of air inside the recorder vibrate. By covering the holes down its shaft with your fingers, you can play different notes.

Some wind instruments, like the clarinet, have metal keys to open or close the holes. Others have a different mouthpiece. The flute has a sideways mouthpiece so it is played sideways.

Put some water in a milk bottle. Blow across the top of the bottle. Can you make a note sound? When you blow across the top, you make the air inside the bottle vibrate so that it makes a sound. Find eight milk bottles and put different amounts of water in each. Can you make an eight-note octave? Try playing a tune with your bottle band.

Our voices

The human voice is a wind instrument worked by breath from the lungs. The air passes over two flaps or membranes in our throat, called the **vocal cords**, making them vibrate. By opening or closing our vocal cords, we can make low sounds and high sounds. We do this automatically.

The quality of our voice comes from the spaces or cavities in our body. They work like the sound box in a guitar. The chest cavity makes deep, rich sounds. The cavities in our head give high, sharp sounds.

To speak or sing, we need to fill our lungs with air and then let it out. A special muscle in our lower chest, called the **diaphragm**, helps. People who sing in operas or musicals, train and develop their diaphragms just as athletes develop other muscles.

Sound travels

Sound travels through air. But sound also travels through solid objects and through liquids. Sound travels at different speeds through different substances. The table shows you some speeds. Through which substances does sound travel fastest and slowest?

Substance	Speed sound travels through substance
Air	1160 kilometres per hour
Lead	4320 kilometres per hour
Water	5400 kilometres per hour
Brass	12 620 kilometres per hour
Steel	18 120 kilometres per hour

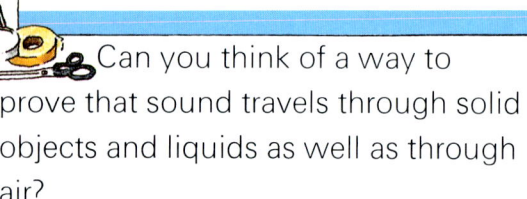

Can you think of a way to prove that sound travels through solid objects and liquids as well as through air?

Whales and dolphins can hear each other. The sounds they make travel for hundreds of kilometres through the sea. The sounds travel much further than they would if they were made out of the water in the open air.

In the Wild West, cowboys used to listen out for approaching trains by putting their ears to the track. When the train was on its way, they could hear the track buzzing with sound before they could hear the train itself. **Never go near a railway track—it is very dangerous**.

Try making a speaking machine using two empty yoghurt pots or tins and a long length of string. Can you use your speaking machine to send a message to a friend without shouting? If you want to send the message around the corner, you will have to make something to hold the string from the wall. You could also try making a code by plucking the string.

If there are any metal railings around your school try sending sound messages down them to friends.

Half Asleep

Half asleep
And half awake
I drift like a boat
On an empty lake
And the sounds in the houses
And street that I hear
Though far away
Sound very clear;
There's my sister Betty
Playing by the stairs
Shouting like teacher
At her teddy bears.

I can hear Mum chatting
To Mrs Spence next door
And I feel the tumbler
Vibrating the floor.
And Alan Simpson
Plays his guitar
And his dad
Keeps trying
To start his car.
Dave, the mechanic
Who's out on strike
Keeps tuning and revving
His Yamaha bike.
From the open window
Across the street
On the August air
Drifts a reggae beat.

In the Kitchen

In the kitchen
After the aimless
Chatter of the plates,
The murmuring of the gas,
The chuckles of the water pipes
And the sharp exchanges
Of the knives, forks and spoons,
Comes the serious quiet
When the sink slowly clears its throat,
And you can hear the occasional rumble
Of the refrigerator's tummy
As it digests the cold.

John Cotton

At four o'clock
With a whoop and a shout
The kids from St. John's
Come tumbling out.
I can hear their shouts
Hear what they say
And I play in my head
All the games they play.

Gareth Owen

The Birdman

Ludwig Koch lived at the beginning of this century. His hobby was collecting bird-songs. When he was a boy, he drew bird-pictures in a notebook. Then, underneath, he wrote down each bird's song. He could read his notes and gave bird-concerts to his family and friends. He showed them his bird-pictures and sang or whistled the songs that went with them.

When Ludwig Koch grew up, he worked for a recording company. The company made records of music. No one had ever thought of recording anything else.

Why don't you record bird-songs? I'm sure people would buy them.

We'll do it. Catch some birds, put them in cages and record their songs.

I can't do that. We don't want records of birds in cages. Birds belong in the open air, flying freely or perching on trees or in bushes. I'll record them in the open air.

The recording company thought that he was crazy. In those days, there were no tape recorders small enough to carry in your pocket. Recording machines were as big as suitcases and three times heavier. Microphones were as big as hot-water bottles. Before you made a recording, you had to spend hours fixing up the machine. You had to hang an aerial from a high branch. You had to unwind many metres of wire and trail it through the undergrowth.

But Ludwig Koch was patient. First, he decided which bird-songs he wanted to record. Then he went for a walk to find where the birds usually sat and sang. When he found a good place, he hurried home to fetch his recording equipment. It filled his car. Wires and poles straggled out of the windows. Ludwig Koch drove back to the place and parked the car.

Then he set up his machine. The job sometimes took all day. When the machine was ready, he covered it with leafy branches, to hide it from the birds. As soon as everything was ready, he sat beside the machine in the shelter to wait for the birds to come.

The birds settled on the branches and began singing. Ludwig Koch switched on his machine and recorded them.

Ludwig Koch's bird-records soon became famous. They let people hear real open-air sounds. When birds sing in the open, there are other noises all round them—the rustle of leaves, the rush of wind, the cracking of twigs and sometimes even cows mooing or dogs barking in the distance. All these sounds were on Ludwig Koch's records. When you heard them, it was like enjoying a country walk in your own sitting-room.

After a few years, Ludwig Koch began playing his records on the radio. He told people about his trips into the countryside to record the birds. Then he played the bird-song records. People nicknamed him 'the Birdman'.

He went on recording birds until he was over 80 years old. He made more bird-recordings than any other person who has ever lived.

High and loud sounds

Many animals have much better hearing than we do. It is hard to imagine how sounds must seem to other creatures. A twig splitting as we step on it, may sound like a crack of thunder to some woodland creatures. It will certainly warn them of approaching danger. Animals make many sounds which we cannot hear at all. Their pitch is too high for our ears. Some dog owners have special whistles which they blow to call their dog. Dogs can hear these whistles but humans cannot.

There are many noises which are unpleasant and even dangerous to our ears. Too great a noise can damage our ears. Such sounds include drills, explosions, aircraft and even too much loud music. People who work in a very noisy environment protect their ears with ear-muffs or headphones.

Loudness scale

The loudness of sound is measured in decibels. This table shows the measurement in decibels of various sounds:

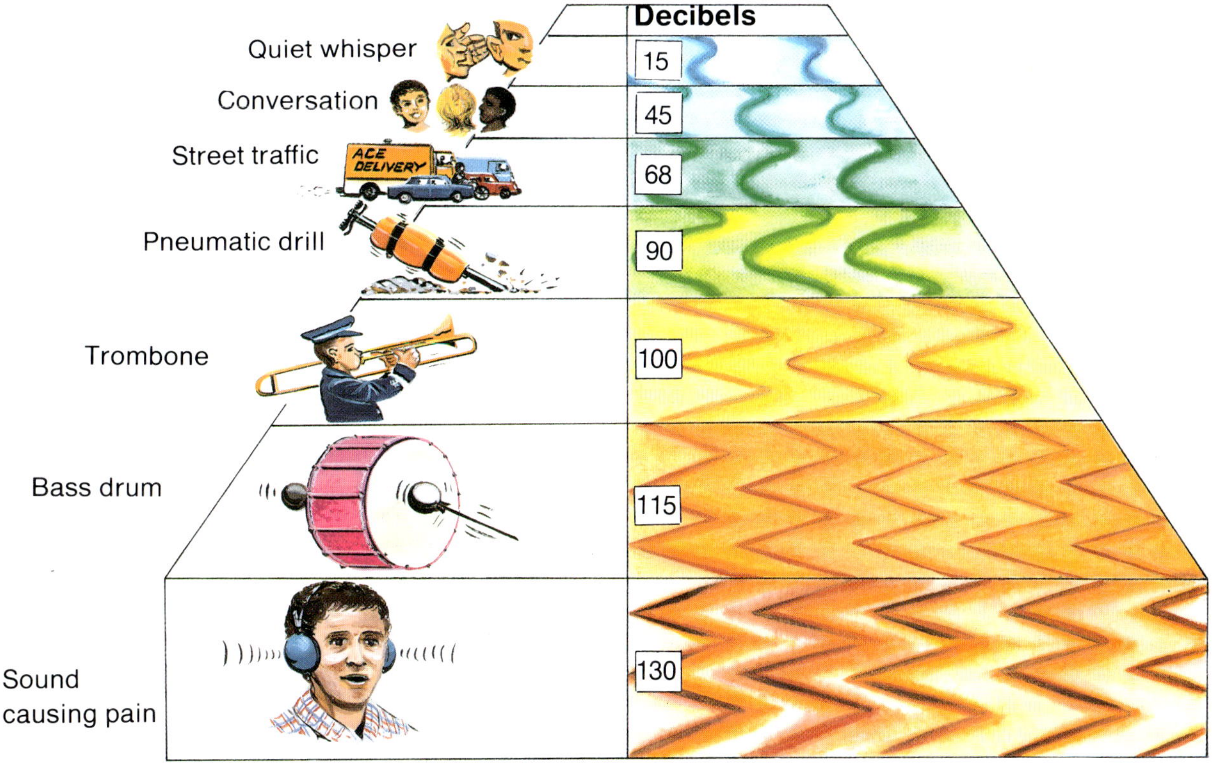

	Decibels
Quiet whisper	15
Conversation	45
Street traffic	68
Pneumatic drill	90
Trombone	100
Bass drum	115
Sound causing pain	130

Can you make your own sound scale from 1 to 10? What would you put at 0? What would you put at 10?

Can you make a loud sound quieter? Make an electric bell or buzzer that makes a loud noise. Put it in a box. Can you stop the sound without turning it off? What can you put in, or around the box to make the sound quieter? You could also try using a clock with a loud tick to make the noise.

Glossary

bow
A rod made of wood and nylon or horsehair which is pulled across the strings of a stringed instrument to produce sounds.

diaphragm
A muscle in the lower chest which helps us breathe.

pitch
Pitch describes how high or low a note is.

sound wave
Sound is made when something vibrates, and sound waves are the movements of those vibrations.

vocal cords
Membranes or flaps in the throat which vibrate and produce a huge variety of sounds.